SPACE

BY RAMAN PRINJA

KINGFISHER

CONTENTS

Zoom through space   6

PLANETS   8
The Solar System   10
Close up: Planet Earth   12
The Earth's Moon   14
Rocky planets   16
Crossing the Asteroid Belt   18
Giant gas planets   20
Top 10: Moons   22
Dwarf planets   24

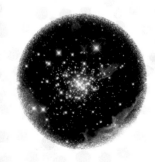

STARS AND GALAXIES   26
Close up: The Sun   28
Stellar night sky   30
Constellations   32

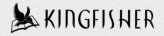

KINGFISHER

First published 2017 by Kingfisher
an imprint of Macmillan Children's Books
20 New Wharf Road, London N1 9RR
Associated companies throughout the world
www.panmacmillan.com

To Kamini, Vikas and Sachin – RP

Series editor: Hayley Down
Design: Jeni Child

ISBN 978-0-7534-4108-4

9 8 7 6 5 4 3 2 1

1TR/0417/WKT/UG/128MA

A CIP catalogue record for this book is available from the British Library.

Printed in China

Picture credits
The Publisher would like to thank the following for permission to reproduce their material.
Top = t; Bottom = b; Middle = m; Left = l; Right = r
Front cover: NASA; Back cover: iStock/Creativemarc; Cover flap: Shutterstock/Egyptian Studio; Page 1 NASA/Hubble; 3 iStock/Ales_Utovko; 4–5, 4t, 4b, 5m NASA; 6 NASA/ESA/Hubble/Judy Schmidt; 7t Alamy/Science Lab; 7m, 7b NASA; 8–9 Alamy/Iuliia Bycheva; 10–11 NASA; 12–13 NASA/Goddard Space Flight Centre; 14–15 iStock/guvendemir; 15 Shutterstock/Quaoar; 16–17 NASA/JPL-Caltech/Cornell Univ./Arizona State Univ.; 16tr NASA/JPL; 16tm NASA/John Hopkins University Applied Physics Laboratory/Carnegie Institution of Washington; 16tml (Messenger) Creative Commons; 16tmr (Cassini) Creative Commons); 16bl NASA/ John Hopkins University Applied Physics Laboratory/Carnegie Institution of Washington and Dr Paolo C. Fienga/LXTT/IPF for the additional process and color; 16brNASA/JPL; 17tl, 17tr, 17bl NASA; 17br NASA/JPL/University of Arizona; 17tm Shutterstock/3Dsculptor; 18–19 NASA/JPL-Calt; 19tr NASA/JHUAPL; 19b NASA/ University of Tennesee; 20tl, 20tr NASA; 20bl, 21tr, 21br, NASA/JPL; 20br NASA/JPL-Caltech/Space Science Institute; 21tl Lawrence Sromovsky, University of Wisconsin-Madison/W.W. Keck Observatory; 21bl Erich Karkoschka (University of Arizona) and NASA; 22 (1) Alamy/NASA/World History Archive & ARPL; 23tl (2), 23tl (3), 23mr (9), 23br (10) Creative Commons; 23ml (4) Shutterstock/Quaoar; 23bl (5) Alamy/World History Archive; 23bl (6), 23tr (8) NASA/JPL/Space Science Institute; 23tr (7) Alamy/World History Archive; 24 NASA; 25t Alamy/NASA Photo; 25m Creative Commons/European Southern Observatory (ESO); 25b NASA; 26–27 NASA, ESA, R. O'Connell (University of Virginia), F. Paresce (National Institute for Astrophysics, Bologna, Italy), E. Young (Universities Space Research Association/Ames Research Center), the WFC3 Science Oversight Committee, and the Hubble Heritage Team (STScI/AURA); 28–29 iStock/solarseven; 30–31 European Space Agency & NASA; 30 ESA/NASA; 31 ESA/Hubble and NASA; 32tr Shutterstock/NikitaRoytman Photography; 32bl NASA; 32br Alamy/Panther Media GmbH; 33bl Shutterstock/igordabari; 33br Alamy/Alan Dyer; 34 (1) NASA/CXC/JPL-Caltech/STScI; 35tl (2) Shutterstock/Egyptian Studio; 35tl (3) 35ml (4), 35bl (5), 35bl (6) 35tr (7), 35mr (9), NASA; 35tr (8) X-ray: NASA/CXC/Rutgers/J.Hughes; Optical: NASA/STScI; 35br (10) NASA/JPL-Caltech; 36tl, 37tl NASA, ESA, the Hubble Heritage Team (STScI/AURA), and R. Gendler (for the Hubble Heritage Team) Acknowledgment: J. GaBany; 36bl (Messier 101) NASA/JPL-Caltech/STScI; 36bl (Galaxy) ESA/Hubble & NASA and N. Gorin (STScI); 36br NASA/CXC/SAO; 37tr X-ray: NASA/CXC/MSU/J.Strader et al, Optical: NASA/STScI; 37br NASA/JPL-Caltech/ SSC; 38 X-ray: NASA/CXC/Penn State/L.Townsley et al, Optical: ESO/2.2m telescope; 39t NASA; 39b iStock/ClaudioVentrella; 40–41 NASA/CXC/SAO/J.DePasquale; IR: NASA/JPL-Caltech; Optical: NASA/STScI; 42 iStock/den-belitsky; 43t NASA/JPL-Caltech/ESA/CXC/STScI; 43m NASA/ESO; 44, 45ml Shutterstock/pixelparticle; 45t NASA/JPL-Caltech/ESA/CXC/STScI; 45ml, 45m NASA/JPL-Caltech 46–47 NASA, ESA, and D. Coe, J. Anderson, and R. van der Marel (STScI); 47 NASA/JPL-Caltech; 48–49 NASA; 50, 51t, 51b NASA; 51m Getty/Corbis; 52 NASA/Bill Ingalls; 53t, 53b NASA; 54–55 NASA/JPL-Caltech/MSSS; 56 (1), 56mr (3), 56br (4), 57ml (5), 57bl (6), 57tr (7), 57mr (9), 59 br (10) NASA; 56bl (2) NASA/JPL-Caltech; 57tr (8) NASA Photo/Lori Losey; 58–59 Alamy/RGB Ventures; 58, 59, 60, 61, 62 NASA; 63 NASA/Hubble.

Top 10: Star stages   34

Galaxy types   36

Our Milky Way Galaxy   38

Close up: Colliding galaxies   40

Galaxy groups   42

The Big Bang   44

The end?   46

EXPLORING SPACE   48

Eyes on the Universe   50

Missions to the planets   52

Close up: Roaming around Mars 54

Top 10: Space missions   56

International Space Station   58

The super space quiz   60

Glossary   62

Index   64

ZOOM THROUGH SPACE

Space is the whole Universe. We think of space as starting from above the Earth's sky and stretching out beyond the Moon, planets, stars and galaxies. The Universe is incredibly vast, with powerful forces and huge energies at work inside it. In this book, we will zoom outwards from the Earth to explore objects that come into view as we move farther and farther out into space ...

stars, gas and dust in space

INSIDE YOU'LL FIND ...

... the Solar System

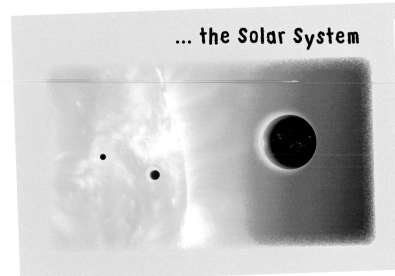

ENERGY is the power needed to make things happen. You use energy to run or walk. Everything in space uses energy too! The Sun uses energy to shine and the planets use energy to orbit the Sun.

Energy can be related to a **FORCE** that can cause movement by pushing or pulling. Gravity is a force that pulls things together. It holds stars together in groups called galaxies, which exist in lots of shapes and sizes.

... spectacular stars and galaxies!

... out-of-this-world explorers!

When measuring distances in space, astronomers use a measurement called a **LIGHT-YEAR**. It is the same as the distance light can travel through space in one year – it equals 9500 billion kilometres. The Milky Way measures 150,000 light-years across.

PLANETS

THE SOLAR SYSTEM

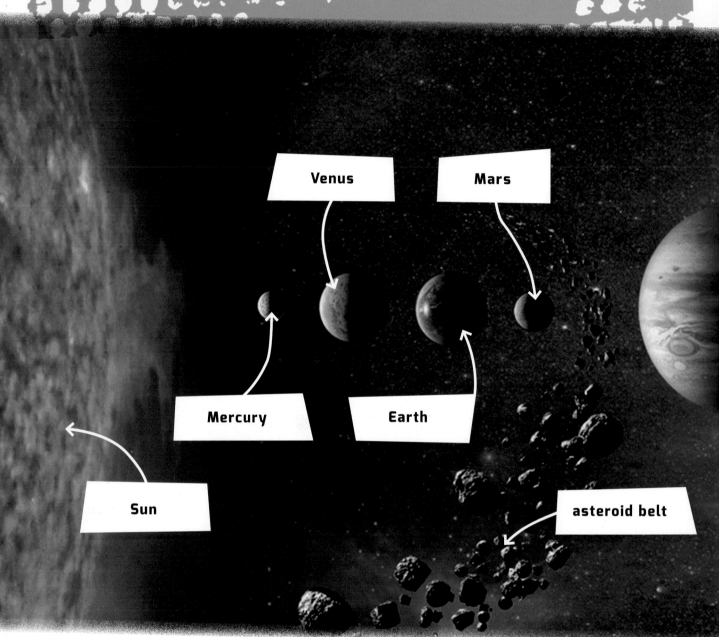

Venus

Mars

Mercury

Earth

Sun

asteroid belt

The Solar System is about 4.6 billion years old. It is made up of our Sun and all the objects circling it along paths called orbits. The Sun is orbited by eight planets, hundreds of moons, millions of asteroids, several **dwarf planets** and lots of space **probes** that people on the Earth have sent into space.

You can remember the order of the planets using this sentence: "My Very Eager Mouse Just Swallowed Up Noodles". The first letter of each word will remind you of the first letter of the correct planet, starting from the Sun: Mercury, Venus, Earth, Mars, Jupiter, Saturn, Uranus, Neptune!

The **OORT CLOUD** is an icy shell that surrounds the Kuiper Belt and all the planets in the Solar System. Astronomers think there may be two trillion cold comets in the Oort cloud.

Jupiter

Uranus

Saturn

Neptune

The **KUIPER BELT** is a region beyond Neptune, which holds trillions of small, icy objects. It stretches up to 50 times the distance between the Earth and the Sun. It is home to dwarf planets and comets.

The Sun contains 99.9 per cent of the Solar System's **MASS**, with Jupiter and Saturn making up most of the rest. Mercury, Venus, Earth and Mars make up a tiny percentage of the Solar System's mass.

CLOSE UP

PLANET EARTH

We live on a small, rocky planet called the Earth, about 150 million kilometres from our nearest star, the Sun. The Earth is very special because it is the only world known to support life. Nearly 70 per cent of the Earth's surface is covered by its oceans of salty water.

Space Shuttle *Atlantis*

More about the Earth:

The Earth has an atmosphere – layers of **gases** around the planet – containing oxygen, the gas you breathe. No other planet in the Solar System has so much oxygen because it is produced by the Earth's trees and other plants.

THE EARTH'S MOON

Your questions about the Moon answered.

How big is the Moon?

The Moon has a **diameter** of 3475 kilometres, which is about a quarter of the size of the Earth. If you imagine the Earth as a basketball, then on this scale the Moon would be a tennis ball placed about 7.4 metres away.

How did the Moon form?

Scientists think the Moon was formed when a Mars-sized object crashed into the Earth about 4.5 billion years ago. The smash threw material from the Earth into orbit. Some of the material crashed back to the Earth, but gravity squeezed the rest together to make the Moon. This idea is known as the giant-impact theory.

crater on the Moon

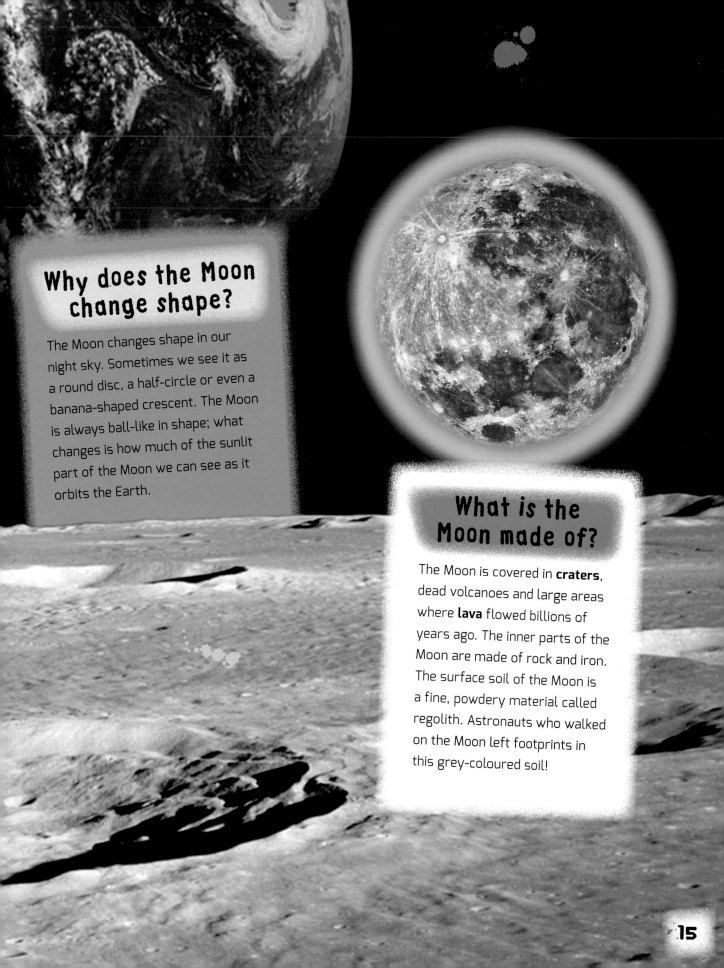

Why does the Moon change shape?

The Moon changes shape in our night sky. Sometimes we see it as a round disc, a half-circle or even a banana-shaped crescent. The Moon is always ball-like in shape; what changes is how much of the sunlit part of the Moon we can see as it orbits the Earth.

What is the Moon made of?

The Moon is covered in **craters**, dead volcanoes and large areas where **lava** flowed billions of years ago. The inner parts of the Moon are made of rock and iron. The surface soil of the Moon is a fine, powdery material called regolith. Astronauts who walked on the Moon left footprints in this grey-coloured soil!

Meet the Earth's neighbours in the Solar System! These relatively small planets are made of mostly rock and metal.

ROCKY

MESSENGER

Venus Express

MERCURY

Next to the Sun, Mercury is about the same size as the Earth's Moon. Its surface is covered in deep, bowl-shaped craters. From day to night, the temperature can go from a scorching 430 degrees Celsius to a freezing –187 degrees Celsius. This is because the planet lacks an atmosphere to keep in the heat. Mercury is the Solar System's fastest planet, orbiting the Sun at 172 kilometres per hour. It has no moons.

craters on Mercury

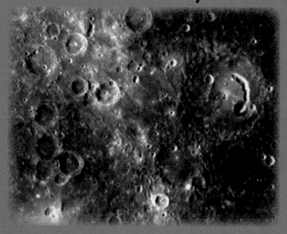

VENUS

The second planet from the Sun, Venus is the Earth's "twin" – the two planets are about the same size! Venus is the brightest planet in our night sky. Its thick atmosphere is made mostly of carbon dioxide, with some clouds made of acid. The surface of Venus has lots of **extinct** volcanoes and lava flowed there billions of years ago. With a surface temperature of 462 degrees Celsius, Venus is the Solar System's hottest planet. It has no moons.

volcano on Venus

PLANETS

International Space Station

Curiosity

EARTH

The Earth is the third planet from the Sun. Like Mercury and Venus, the Earth has a rocky surface with mountains and deep canyons. Unlike other rocky planets, the Earth has volcanoes that are still active today. The Earth's **continents** sit on rocky plates that move to cause **earthquakes**. The Earth is the only rocky planet in the Solar System with oceans of water on its surface.

mountains on the Earth

MARS

Mars is the farthest rocky planet from the Sun. It is sometimes known as the "Red Planet" due to the rusty iron material that covers its surface. Mars has the largest mountain in the Solar System, known as Olympus Mons. At 22 kilometres tall, it is nearly three times taller than Mount Everest on the Earth. The atmosphere of Mars is mostly made of carbon dioxide. Mars has two moons, called Phobos and Deimos.

frosted dunes on Mars

Billions of
ASTEROIDS
are found in a region
between Mars and
Jupiter called the
Asteroid Belt.

CROSSING THE
ASTEROID
BELT

Asteroids are small, rocky
objects that orbit the Sun.
Studying asteroids can teach
us how the planets formed.

The **ASTEROID BELT** is so vast that
the distance between asteroids is on average
966,000 kilometres. This means spacecraft
can fly through the asteroid belt without
crashing into anything!

Asteroids are made of **ROCK**, **STONE**
and **METAL**. Some asteroids are very
solid, while others are lumps of rubble
loosely held together by gravity.

The **LARGEST** asteroid, Ceres, is
950 kilometres in diameter. It is also
known as a dwarf planet.

In 2001, **EROS** became the first asteroid to have a space probe land on it successfully.

There are **200 OBJECTS** that are more than 100 kilometres in diameter in the Asteroid Belt, and almost one million asteroids that are over one kilometre across.

In 2011, the **DAWN SPACECRAFT** mission became the first-ever spacecraft to go into orbit around an asteroid in the Asteroid Belt.

The huge force of **JUPITER'S** gravity stopped objects in the Asteroid Belt from coming together to make a small planet.

The **TOTAL MASS** of the Asteroid Belt is less than that of the Earth's Moon.

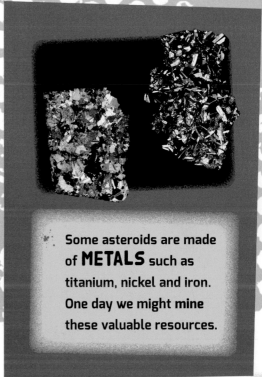

Some asteroids are made of **METALS** such as titanium, nickel and iron. One day we might **mine** these valuable resources.

There is a huge jump in distance between Mars, the last rocky planet, and Jupiter, the first of the gas giants.

GIANT

JUPITER

Diameter: 142,984 km
Mass: 318 Earths
Distance from Sun: 778.6 million km
Rings: 4 main
Moons: 67 known
Atmosphere: hydrogen, helium, methane
Rotation period: 9.9 hours
Temperature at top layers: −108°C

The Great Red Spot is a storm on Jupiter's surface; it is twice as wide as the Earth. In fact 1321 planet Earths would fit inside Jupiter!

Jupiter's Great Red Spot

SATURN

Diameter: 120,536 km
Mass: 95 Earths
Distance from Sun: 1434 million km
Rings: more than 30
Moons: 62 known
Atmosphere: hydrogen, helium, methane
Rotation period: 10.7 hours
Temperature at top layers: −139°C

Saturn has storms that can last for six months, firing lightning bolts 10,000 times more powerful than those on the Earth!

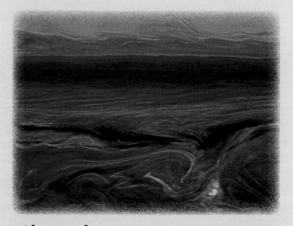

lightning storm on Saturn

GAS PLANETS

URANUS

Diameter: 51,118 km
Mass: 15 Earths
Distance from Sun: 2873 million km
Rings: 13 main
Moons: 27 known
Atmosphere: hydrogen, helium, methane
Rotation period: 17.2 hours
Temperature at top layers: −197°C

The **poles** of Uranus are on its sides, not the top and the bottom. This makes it look like the planet is rolling around the Sun on its side.

sideways Uranus

NEPTUNE

Diameter: 49,528 km
Mass: 17 Earths
Distance from Sun: 4495 million km
Rings: 5 main
Moons: 14 known
Atmosphere: hydrogen, helium, methane
Rotation period: 16.1 hours
Temperature at top layers: −201°C

Neptune's atmosphere is made up of swirling clouds of a gas called methane. This gas gives the planet its bright-blue colour.

gassy Neptune!

MOONS

There are 181 known moons in the Solar System, but which are the most interesting?

1 Io

Pronounced "eye-oh", this moon orbits Jupiter. Its surface is covered with hundreds of volcanoes, some of which erupt with such power that lava shoots tens of kilometres into the air.

2 Triton

This is the only moon in the Solar System to have a **retrograde orbit** – it orbits in the opposite direction to its planet's rotation.

3 Phobos

Mars' largest moon is on a **collision course**! In 50 million years, it will crash into Mars or break up to form a ring. Look out!

4 Luna

Luna was the Roman name for the Earth's Moon. We use "lunar" to describe things to do with the Moon, such as the lunar landing.

5 Callisto

One of Jupiter's moons, Callisto has more craters than any other object in the Solar System!

6 Iapetus

Orbiting Saturn, Iapetus is sometimes called the "yin and yang" moon. One side of its surface is very dark; the other is very light.

7 Ganymede

This is the biggest moon in the Solar System! Ganymede has oxygen in its atmosphere, but not enough for you to live there.

8 Enceladus

One of Saturn's moons, Enceladus has a surface of ice that reflects light. An enormous ocean lies under this ice-crust.

9 Europa

There is more water below the surface of Jupiter's moon Europa than there is in all of the Earth's oceans put together.

10 Titan

Saturn's largest moon has a thick atmosphere of gases. These gases give Titan its bright-orange colour.

Which moon would you like to travel to?

DWARF PLANETS

In 2006, astronomers came up with a new term: dwarf planet. This is the name for an object that is smaller than a normal planet and ball-shaped, but is not a moon in orbit around another planet. Unlike a true planet, a dwarf planet's orbit around the Sun is littered with pieces of rock and other bodies.

COSMIC FACT

In addition to the eight main planets, there are five known **DWARF PLANETS** in the Solar System. The dwarf planets are called Ceres, Pluto, Haumen, Makemake and Eris. There may be hundreds more dwarf planets waiting to be discovered!

Ceres

Pluto

PLUTO is the largest known dwarf planet with a diameter of 2372 kilometres. The smallest dwarf planet, Ceres, is 950 kilometres across.

Eris

The farthest dwarf planet from the Sun, **ERIS** takes 560 years to complete just one orbit round the Sun.

Pluto's surface

In July 2015, the NASA **SPACECRAFT** *New Horizons* made the first visit to Pluto. It sent us images of craters, cliffs and valleys on Pluto's surface. It also sent close-ups of Pluto's five tiny moons!

STARS AND GALAXIES

THE SUN

The Sun is our nearest star. Made of mostly hot hydrogen and helium gases, it provides the Earth with the right amount of heat and light to make life possible. The Sun's mass gives it an enormous gravity, which keeps the planets of the Solar System in orbit around it. The Sun's diameter is 1.4 million kilometres; the Earth would fit inside it over one million times! Light takes 8 minutes to travel from the Sun to the Earth.

More about the Sun:

The Sun has a changing **magnetic field**, which makes it very active. Sometimes this activity is visible as dark patches, called sunspots, and explosive flares. **Aurorae** (such as the Northern Lights) appear in the Earth's night sky when material thrown off by the Sun strikes the Earth's atmosphere.

STELLAR NIGHT SKY

Your questions about spectacular stars answered!

Why do stars twinkle?

Stars twinkle because the air in the Earth's atmosphere is moving around. This movement is called turbulence. The shifting air bends the light's path as it travels from a star to our eyes. From outside our atmosphere, a star's shine is constant, not twinkly!

Why are stars different colours?

If you look carefully, you should see that stars in the night sky are not all the same colour. There are some reddish, orange and blue stars, along with lots of white and yellow ones. The stars have different colours because their outer layers (the photospheres) have different temperatures. Red stars are cooler than blue ones.

Why are some stars brighter than others?

There are bright and dim stars because some stars are much closer to the Earth than others, making them appear much brighter. Stars also have different brightnesses because some of them are more powerful and give off a lot more light. Older stars may become small and dim.

Where do the stars go during the day?

During daytime, the stars *are* still in the sky! You cannot see them because the light from the Sun is so bright. Sunlight is spread across our sky by the Earth's atmosphere, making it too bright to see the fainter stars in the sky.

CONSTELLATIONS

AQUILA: THE EAGLE

Aquila is easiest to spot during summer in the northern **hemisphere**. In Greek mythology Aquila, "the Eagle", served the god Zeus, sending messages down to the Earth. Zeus was so pleased with Aquila's actions that he placed the Eagle among the stars to fly forever through the sky.

CASSIOPEIA: THE QUEEN

Cassiopeia is an easy constellation to look for in the autumn skies of the northern hemisphere. In ancient myths, Cassiopeia was a queen known for her great beauty. However, she was punished for boasting about how beautiful she was, and so the gods forced Cassiopeia to remain in the sky tied to a chair.

Constellations are patterns drawn using the stars –
like dot-to-dot puzzles! Ancient people named them
after characters from their myths and legends. Today,
astronomers use 88 constellations to map the night sky.

CYGNUS:
THE SWAN

Cygnus is one of the brightest
constellations. It can be seen from June
to December in the northern hemisphere
and in the winter months in the southern
hemisphere. One Ancient Greek myth says
that Zeus once disguised himself as a swan
to take Queen Leda under his wings and save
her when she was attacked by an eagle.

ORION:
THE HUNTER

Orion is a great constellation to look
out for in the northern hemisphere
during November–February. Two of the
brightest 10 stars in the night sky, Rigel
and Betelgeuse, are in this constellation. In
Greek mythology, Orion was a great hunter
and the son of Poseidon, the sea god. He
hunted to provide the gods with food.

TOP 10 STAR STAGES

Stars don't live forever! They have life cycles that last billions of years.

1 A star in the making

Stars are born in clouds called nebulae, made of mostly hydrogen and helium gases.

2 A star is born

Inside a nebula, matter is squeezed tightly by gravity, becoming very hot. This forms the star.

7 Massive stars

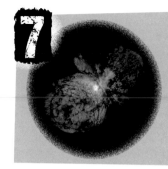

Stars that are born with much more mass than the Sun have a much shorter life cycle. They are called massive stars.

3 Long lives

Stars live for ages! The Sun will last for about 10 billion years. It is currently halfway through its life cycle.

8 Supernovae

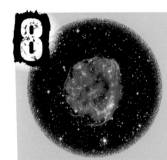

Massive stars die in explosions called supernovae.

4 Out of energy

All stars die when their supply of **nuclear energy** runs out and they cannot shine anymore.

9 Black holes

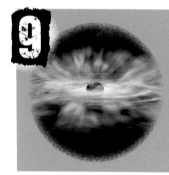

A supernova can leave behind a very strange thing: a black hole! Its gravity is so strong that even light cannot escape it.

5 Planetary nebulae

About five billion years from now, the Sun will die by throwing out gas to make a **planetary nebula**.

10 New stars

The matter thrown out in a supernova explosion spreads out in space and may be recycled to make new stars.

6 White dwarfs

The final stage in a star's death will come when it is squeezed by gravity to make an Earth-sized star, called a white dwarf.

Which star stage is the most fascinating?

Galaxy M106

GALAXY

A galaxy is a group of billions of stars and clouds of gas and dust held together by gravity. The Solar System is in a galaxy called the Milky Way. There are four main types of galaxy ...

SPIRAL

A spiral galaxy looks like a pinwheel. The central part of the galaxy is a large bulge of lots of tightly packed stars. Arms made of young stars and dust spiral outwards from the bulge. Our Milky Way galaxy is a spiral galaxy. This type of galaxy contains lots of young and old stars.

Messier 101

ELLIPTICAL

Elliptical galaxies are oval or egg-shaped. They don't have arms. These galaxies contain mostly very old stars and not many new stars are being made inside them. Some of the largest galaxies in the Universe are elliptical. They can span one million light-years across.

Centaurus A

TYPES

Sombrero

NGC 4649

LENTICULAR

A lenticular galaxy is mid-way between a spiral and an elliptical galaxy. It has an egg-shaped bulge in the middle and very faint arms that are tightly wound around its centre. These galaxies are normally much brighter than spiral galaxies.

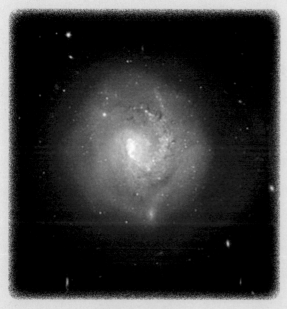

MRK 820

IRREGULAR

Irregular galaxies have no clear shape or pattern. They are small galaxies with many clouds of gas and dust inside them. Lots of new stars are being made in irregular galaxies. This can make the galaxies very bright.

IC 1613

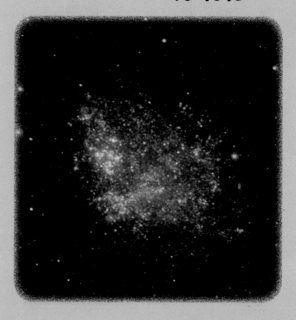

Clouds of gas and dust in the Sagittarius spiral arm of the Milky Way Galaxy

The Milky Way Galaxy is an incredible **13.5 BILLION** years old.

OUR MILKY WAY GALAXY

Find out incredible facts about our home galaxy!

- There is a super-massive **BLACK HOLE** at the centre of our Galaxy. The black hole has a mass of about four million Suns!

- The Milky Way Galaxy is very flat. It is **100,000** light-years in diameter, but only a few thousand light-years thick.

- The Galaxy is surrounded by a halo, which contains a mysterious type of **matter**, called **DARK MATTER**. You cannot directly see dark matter through a telescope.

The Milky Way Galaxy is made up of **200 BILLION** stars!

The **MILKY WAY** gets its name from a fuzzy white band of stars that you can see stretching across the sky at night. This is our view of it from inside the Galaxy.

COLLIDING GALAXIES

Sometimes galaxies can be squeezed so close together that they crash into each other! In this image from the Hubble Space Telescope, you can see two spiral galaxies, called NGC 4038 and NGC 4039, colliding. They are about 45 million light-years away from the Earth.

NGC 4038

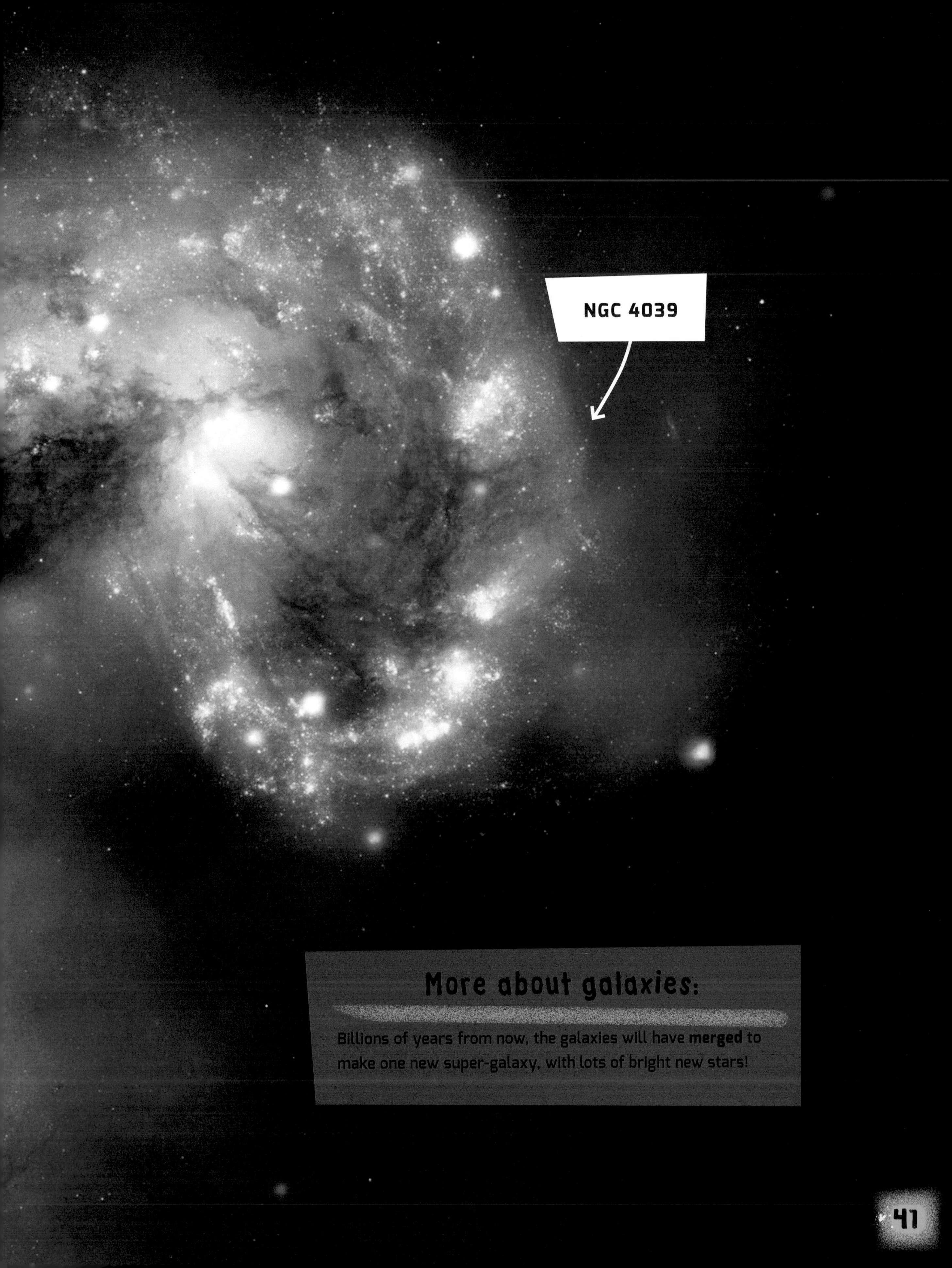

NGC 4039

More about galaxies:

Billions of years from now, the galaxies will have **merged** to make one new super-galaxy, with lots of bright new stars!

GALAXY GROUPS

A galaxy group is a collection of a few tens of galaxies, brought together by gravity into an area that measures a few million light-years across.

The Milky Way belongs to the Local Group, which contains about 50 galaxies crowded together into a space with a diameter of 10 million light-years!

The Arp 273 grouping of galaxies is about 300 million light-years away from the Earth.

galaxies in Virgo cluster

GALAXY CLUSTERS are **LARGER** structures containing a few hundred galaxies packed into a region that measures a few million light-years across. The Local Group is brought together with other galaxy groups to make a galaxy cluster called Virgo.

supercluster

SUPERCLUSTERS are even larger collections of galaxies! They can extend over a few 100 million light-years and bring together many clusters. The Virgo cluster is found inside a supercluster called **LANIAKEA**.

Your home address may be written as: house, street, town or city, county, country, continent. Now you can write your address in the Universe too! Here it is:

**PLANET EARTH,
SOLAR SYSTEM,
MILKY WAY GALAXY,
LOCAL GROUP,
VIRGO CLUSTER,
LANIAKEA SUPERCLUSTER**

THE BIG BANG

Most scientists believe the Universe was born about 13.8 billion years ago in an incredibly large explosion of energy called the Big Bang. In a very tiny fraction of a second, a huge amount of energy was produced. At this time, the Universe was very small and extremely hot. Time, space and matter all began with the Big Bang.

COSMIC FACT

In just a fraction of a second after the Big Bang, the Universe **GREW** in size from smaller than a single atom to bigger than a galaxy!

the Big Bang

early stars

COSMIC FACT

When the Universe was **ONE SECOND** old, tiny particles began to form. After three minutes, the Universe was cool enough for the particles to come together to make the centres of atoms. About 380,000 years later, the Universe cooled enough for complete atoms to form. All matter in the Universe is made up of atoms. The first stars were made 100 million years after the Big Bang.

how the Universe grows

COSMIC FACT

The Universe **GREW RAPIDLY** after the Big Bang and has kept on growing at an amazing rate. It is still expanding (getting bigger) today. You can think of the expanding Universe as a little like blowing up a balloon. All the galaxies that formed would be like dots drawn on the balloon, and they are all moving away from each other as the balloon gets larger and larger.

THE END?

Your questions about the end of the Universe answered!

What is the Big Rip?

The Big Rip **model** suggests that a mysterious type of energy, called dark energy, takes over and pushes the Universe apart very rapidly. This energy acts against gravity and tears apart all the galaxies and stars.

Do we know how the Universe will end?

Scientists are not sure exactly how the Universe will change in the future. They are studying how much mass and energy exist in the Universe. This will help them to understand whether the Universe will carry on expanding forever or if it might collapse on itself. There are a few possible ways the Universe might end ...

What *is* the Big Crunch?

In the Big Crunch model, the Universe stops expanding and then starts to contract (get smaller). As the Universe shrinks, all the galaxies are crushed back together. At the end, all matter in the Universe will collapse into the biggest-ever black hole!

What is the Big Freeze?

Another possibility is that the Universe will carry on expanding forever. All matter, such as galaxies, will be pushed farther apart. Slowly, all of the heat of the Universe will spread very thinly across space. In the end, everything will become cold and dark.

EXPLORING
SPACE

EYES ON THE UNIVERSE

The Universe is incredibly vast and the stars and galaxies are very far away. This means that the light reaching us from objects in space is very faint, just the way the headlights of a car would be very dim at night if the car was far away from you. To learn about galaxies, stars and planets, astronomers collect the light from them using large telescopes.

COSMIC FACT

The **HUBBLE SPACE TELESCOPE** is one of the most successful telescopes ever. It is in orbit about 590 kilometres above the Earth. Working above the atmosphere, it has a much clearer view of the Universe.

Hubble Space Telescope

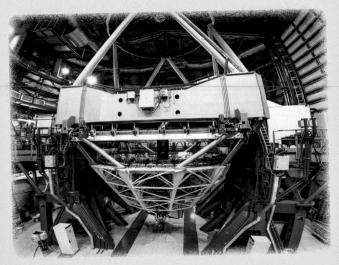

mirror telescope

Most telescopes use light-collecting **MIRRORS** to act as eyes on the Universe. The bigger the telescope, the more light is collected, making the image a lot clearer. Astronomers use giant telescopes with mirrors that are many metres in diameter.

COSMIC FACT

The 10-metre-wide **KECK** telescopes in Hawaii, USA are so powerful they could detect a light as small as the flame of a candle placed at a distance as far as the Moon!

Keck telescope

VLT

COSMIC FACT

The **VLT** (Very Large Telescope) array in Chile allow astronomers to view objects that are four billion times fainter than we can see with our eyes alone.

NASA's latest mission to Jupiter is called **JUNO**. It was launched in 2011 aboard the powerful *Atlas V* rocket and arrived at the planet in 2016.

MISSIONS
TO THE PLANETS

Amazing discoveries have been made by sending spacecraft to explore the Solar System. Here are some fantastic missions:

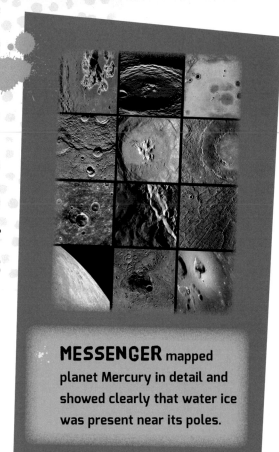

MESSENGER mapped planet Mercury in detail and showed clearly that water ice was present near its poles.

- In July 2015, NASA's **NEW HORIZONS** spacecraft made the first-ever visit to the dwarf planet Pluto. It took more than nine years to travel the 4.8 billion kilometres to reach the planet.

- Launched in March 2004 by the European Space Agency, the **ROSETTA** mission was flown to a comet called 67P/Churyumov–Gerasimenko. In August 2014, the spacecraft went into orbit around the comet. It even landed a probe to explore the comet's rugged surface.

- **MESSENGER** was the first-ever spacecraft to orbit the innermost planet Mercury. It arrived at the rocky planet on 17 March 2011. To end the mission on 30 April 2015, the spacecraft was deliberately slammed into the surface of the planet, carving out a small new crater.

- Orbiting Jupiter, **JUNO** has beamed back photos of violent storms swirling around the planet's north and south poles.

NEW HORIZONS sent back close-ups of valleys and cliffs on Pluto's surface. We also got views of Pluto's five tiny moons!

CLOSE UP

ROAMING AROUND MARS

Curiosity is like a moving laboratory, full of scientific experiments. It has 17 cameras, a scoop to gather and study dust, and it even has a laser and drill to blast rocks and see what they are made of! The data beamed back by *Curiosity* are helping scientists learn about whether Mars could have supported life forms in the past ... or even today!

More about Curiosity:

This is a "selfie" of NASA's *Curiosity* rover on the surface of Mars. *Curiosity* is a car-sized vehicle that arrived on Mars in August 2012. It is remotely controlled from the Earth and has been exploring the planet for the past few years.

TOP 10

SPACE
MISSIONS

Discover the top 10 space exploration missions so far!

1 Spacewalks

In 2001, astronauts Jim Voss and Susan Helms spent the longest time working on a spacewalk. They spent 8 hours and 56 minutes working outside the International Space Station.

3 Odyssey

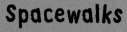

The longest working orbiting spacecraft is *Odyssey*. It has completed more than 60,000 orbits round Mars.

2 Voyager 1

The most distant spacecraft from us is *Voyager 1*. It is now travelling in **interstellar space**, almost 19 billion kilometres away!

4 Opportunity

Opportunity is the longest-surviving rover. It has been travelling and working on the surface of Mars since January 2005.

7 Apollo 17

Astronauts Eugene Cernan and Harrison Schmitt spent the longest time on the Moon: 22 hours 5 minutes and 4 seconds.

8 Discovery

The most used spacecraft is Space Shuttle *Discovery*. It launched the telescope Hubble and helped to build the International Space Station. Wow!

9 Saturn V

NASA's *Saturn V* rocket is the most powerful rocket used so far. It was used to launch the Apollo missions to the Moon.

5 Hayabusa

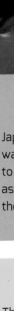

Japan's *Hayabusa* mission was the first spacecraft to collect dust from an asteroid and return it to the Earth.

10 ISS

The International Space Station is the largest structure humans have ever put into space. It is almost 110 metres wide!

6 Juno

The fastest spacecraft is *Juno*, which whizzed towards Jupiter at 265,500 kilometres per hour. It used engines and the pull of gravity.

Where in space would you like to explore?

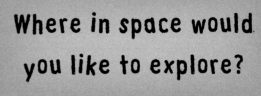

INTERNATIONAL SPACE STATION

Your questions about life aboard the ISS answered!

What is the ISS?

The International Space Station (ISS) is a space laboratory that is in low orbit around the Earth. Astronauts from around the world live and work there. The ISS is powered by enormous solar arrays (solar panels), which produce enough energy to power 40 homes on the Earth.

What do astronauts eat in space?

Space food has come in many forms over the years, from squeezy tubes of liquid to cubes of dried food. Now, it usually comes pre-made in packets – a bit like camping food – that can be warmed up in the ISS oven. There is a huge menu, with 72 types of food to choose from!

What do astronauts do on the ISS?

Astronauts go to the ISS to conduct experiments, carry out research and make repairs. In their spare time, they can watch movies, read and phone their family. There is even gym equipment so they can keep fit!

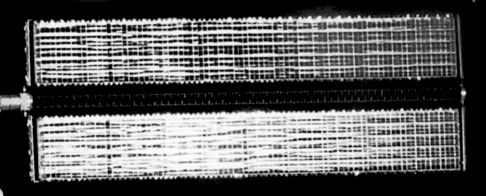

How do astronauts train for the ISS?

Astronauts train hard before shooting into space! They prepare for microgravity in water tanks, they practise living in cramped conditions and they even have language lessons, so they can speak to the Russian Mission Control Centre!

International Space Station

THE SUPER SPACE quiz

Are you an expert on all things space? Test your knowledge by completing this quiz! When you've answered all of the questions, turn to page 63 to check your answer.

 1 Name the telescope that is in orbit around the Earth.
a) Bubble
b) Hubble
c) Trouble

 2 What does ISS stand for?
a) International Space Station
b) International Space Stop
c) International Solar Spot

 3 What is it called when an astronaut leaves the ISS to work outside in open space?
a) Spacewalk
b) Space wander
c) Space stroll

 4 How old is the Solar System?
a) 4.6 thousand years
b) 4.6 million years
c) 4.6 billion years

 5 Which is the only planet that is known to have life on it?
a) Mars
b) Earth
c) Pluto

 6 If you imagine the Earth as a basketball, which sports ball would the Moon be on this scale?
a) Tennis ball
b) Volleyball
c) Ping-pong ball

 7 What are stars made of?
a) Mostly hydrogen and helium gases
b) Mostly lava
c) Mostly rock and ice

 8 A red star seen in the night sky is ...
a) cooler than a blue star
b) hotter than a blue star
c) the same temperature as a blue star

 9 5) How long is the life-cycle of the Sun?
a) 10 hundred thousand years
b) 10 million years
c) 10 billion years

How many Earths would fit inside Jupiter?
a) 103
b) 1321
c) 1 million

 How many dwarf planets are currently known in the Solar System?
a) 1
b) 3
c) 5

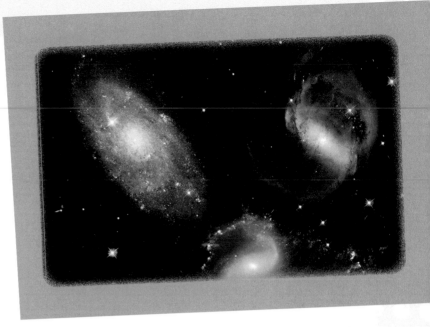

 Where do we find most of the comets in the Solar System?
a) Oort cloud
b) Sort cloud
c) Port cloud

 How long does it take light to travel from the Sun to the Earth?
a) 8 minutes
b) 6 minutes
c) 4 minutes

 What is happening to the two galaxies called NGC 4038 and NGC 4039?
a) They are crashing into each other
b) They are moving away from each other
c) They are orbiting each other

 What type of galaxy is our Milky Way Galaxy?
a) Spiral
b) Elliptical
c) Irregular

 How old is the Universe?
a) 13.8 billion years
b) 12 billion years
c) 11 billion years

 How many stars are there in our Galaxy?
a) 200 billion
b) 20 billion
c) 2 billion

 The Universe today is ...
a) Contracting
b) Expanding
c) Staying still

 What type of object is found at the centre of our Galaxy?
a) A supermassive black hole
b) A star
c) A wormhole

What is the name of a universe where everything collapses and gets squeezed together in the future?
a) The Big Crunch
b) The Big Hunch
c) The Big Lunch

GLOSSARY

atom
A tiny particle. Everthing in the Universe is made up of atoms.

aurora
A display of coloured light seen in the sky when particles from the Sun enter the Earth's atmosphere.

collision course
When two bodies in space are going to crash into each other.

continent
A large mass of land. The Earth's continents are: Africa, Antarctica, Asia, Europe, North America, Oceania and South America.

crater
A bowl-shaped hole made by an object from space hitting the surface of a planet or moon.

diameter
The length of a straight line passing through the centre of a circle. The line connects two points on the edge of the circle.

dwarf planet
A ball-shaped object that is smaller than a normal planet, but is not a moon in orbit around another planet.

earthquake
A violent shaking felt on the Earth's surface, caused by sudden movements of its continents.

extinct (volcano)
No longer erupting and not likely to do so in the future.

gas
A form of matter that is not liquid or solid. The air you breathe is made of gases.

mine
To dig out coal, metals, and other natural materials from the surface of a planet or other space body.

model
A scientific idea about how something works.

nuclear energy
Energy released from the centre of an atom

planetary nebula
A cloud of gas seen surrounding Sun-like stars when they begin to die.

pole
The point at either end of the invisible line known as the axis, around which a planet spins.

probe
A spacecraft that explores space.

retrograde orbit
The path of an object in a clockwise direction when viewed from an imaginary point above the Solar System.

gravity
The force that attracts bodies towards each other. The greater a body's mass, the greater its pull of gravity.

hemisphere
The half of the Earth (or planet) between the north or south pole and the equator.

interstellar space
The gas and dust that exist in the space between the stars.

Kuiper Belt
A large ring of icy objects in our Solar System, beyond Neptune.

lava
Hot, molten rock that erupts onto the surface of a planet and starts to flow.

magnetic field
The lines of force that surround a permanent magnet or moving electric particles.

merged
When two bodies (such as galaxies) come together and make a new, more massive body.

QUIZ ANSWERS: 1 = b, 2 = a, 3 = a, 4 = c, 5 = b, 6 = a, 7 = a, 8 = a, 9 = c, 10 = b, 11 = c, 12 = a, 13 = a, 14 = a, 15 = a, 16 = a, 17 = a, 18 = a, 19 = b, 20 = a.

INDEX

A

Asteroid Belt 10, 18–19
asteroids 10, 18–19, 57
astronauts 15, 56, 57, 58–59
atmospheres 13, 16, 17, 20, 21, 23, 29, 31
atoms 45
aurorae 29

B

Big Bang 44–45
Big Crunch 47
Big Rip 46
black holes 35, 39, 47

C

Callisto 23
carbon dioxide 16, 17
Ceres 18, 24, 25
comets 11, 53
constellations 32–33
craters 15, 16, 23, 25, 53

D, E

dark matter 39
Deimos 17
Earth 10, 11, 12–13, 14, 16, 17, 28, 29
Enceladus 23
energy 7, 35, 44, 46, 58
    dark energy 46
Eris 25
Eros 19
Europa 23

G

galaxies 7, 36–43, 45, 46, 47, 50
    clusters and superclusters 43
    collision 40–41
    groups 42–43
    types 36–37
Ganymede 23
gases 13, 16, 17, 20, 21, 23, 28, 34
gravity 7, 14, 18, 19, 28, 35, 46, 57
Great Red Spot 20

H, I, J

Hubble Space Telescope 40, 50, 57
Iapetus 23
International Space Station (ISS) 56, 57, 58–59
Io 22
Jupiter 11, 19, 20, 22, 23, 53

K, L

Kuiper Belt 11
life forms 12, 28, 54
light-years 7, 36, 39, 40, 42, 43
Luna 23

M

magnetic field 29
Mars 10, 11, 17, 23, 54–55, 56
mass 11, 19, 28, 39, 46
Mercury 10, 11, 16, 53
metals 18, 19
methane 20, 21
Milky Way 7, 36, 38–39, 42
Moon 14–15, 19, 57
moons 17, 20, 21, 22–23, 25, 53
mountains 17

N, O

nebulae 34, 35
Neptune 11, 21
Oort Cloud 11
orbits 7, 10, 14, 15, 16, 19, 25, 28, 53, 56, 58
    retrograde orbit 23
oxygen 13, 23

P

Phobos 17, 23
planets 7, 8–25, 28
    dwarf planets 10, 11, 18, 24–25
    giant gas planets 20–21
    rings 20, 21
    rocky planets 16–17
Pluto 25, 53

R, S

regolith 15
Saturn 11, 20, 23
Solar System 10, 11, 13, 36
space missions 19, 25, 52–57
space shuttles 12–13, 57
spacecraft 10, 18, 19, 25, 52–59
spacewalks 56
stars 7, 26–43, 46, 50
    brightness 31
    colours 30
    constellations 32–33
    galaxies 7, 36–43, 45, 46, 47, 50
    life-cycles 34–35
    twinkling 30
    white dwarfs 35
storms 20, 53
Sun 7, 10, 11, 16, 25, 28–29, 31, 35
sunspots 29
supernovae 35

T

telescopes 40, 50–51, 57
temperatures 16, 20, 21
Titan 23
Triton 23

U

Universe 6, 50
    beginning of 44–45
    end of 46–47
    expansion of 45, 46, 47
Uranus 11, 21

V, W

Venus 10, 11, 16
volcanoes 15, 16, 17, 22
water 12, 17, 23, 53